The Devil's Daughter

written by
Rebecca Rijsdijk

The Devil's Daughter
©Sunday Mornings at the River, 2025
ISBN: 9789083389387

All Rights Reserved.

Sunday Mornings at the River supports copyright as we believe this fuels creativity and promotes free speech.

Thank you for complying with the copyright laws by not reproducing, scanning, or distributing any part of it in any form without permission, except for the purpose of review and promotion of the work.

Poetry by Rebecca Rijsdijk
rebeccarijsdijk.com

Cover image by Julia Margaret Cameron

Sunday Mornings at the River
sundaymorningsattheriver.com

The publisher does not have any control over and does not assume any responsibility for author or third party websites and their content.

Thanks for reading.

*for the rebels
and the poets*

"I am deliberate and afraid of nothing."

— *Audre Lorde*

Contents

Introduction..08
The Devil's Daughter..11
The First Step...13
The Chosen Ones..16
Waiting for Thunder..18
The Rib..20
Exile...22
Dirty Jehovah..24
Field Service..26
The Clothes They Chose...29
The Seat of Power...31
The Marketplace..33
The Hymns at His Funeral..35
The Bottle and the Book...37
The Unholy Boyfriend...39
The Sin of Skin..41
The Ginger Bride...43
The In-Between...45
The Price of Faith..47
The Child They Let Go...49
Her Fall, My Shame..51
Not a Vegetarian..53
Not a Stupid Man..55
The Boy in the Car..57

The Mould	59
The Last Question	61
The Fall	63
What Was Taken	65
No Guidebook	68
The First Candle	70
Waiting for the End	72
Her Return	74
The Stake	76
The Dent in the Mould	78
Ode to the Rebel	81
Why Not a Woman?	83
The Ginger Kid	85
Becoming	87
Epilogue	89
A Note for Those Still Inside	92
About the Author	94
About the Publisher	95

Introduction

I grew up in a world that demanded certainty. The answers were given before the questions could form, and doubt was a sin whispered about in meetings but never confronted directly. As a child in the faith of Jehovah's Witnesses, I was told we were special—chosen to inherit a paradise the rest of the world could never touch. But even as I recited scriptures and knocked on doors, I couldn't shake the feeling that I didn't truly belong.

Being different wasn't safe. It meant standing apart from both the congregation and the world beyond it. We didn't celebrate birthdays, Christmas, or any joy that couldn't be traced directly to God. At school, I was marked as other—a "dirty Jehovah" who wasn't allowed to join the celebrations. Inside the Kingdom Hall, I felt just as distant, my questioning nature branding me as rebellious, dangerous. "Satan's child," my mother called me, not with malice, but with a weariness that spoke of a lifetime of unmet expectations.

Despite the rules, the hymns, and the endless meetings, I knew I didn't fit. I saw through the stories they told us— the Eve and Adam fable that demanded obedience, the apocalyptic visions that stoked fear, and the rigid mould they tried to shape me into. I wanted to run, but I also wanted to stay. Leaving the faith wasn't just walking away from doctrine; it was walking away from my family, my childhood, and the fragile threads of belonging that tethered me to something familiar.

The poems in this collection are fragments of that journey. They begin in the small, controlled world of my childhood, where every decision felt like it had eternal consequences. They trace my years of questioning, of rebellion, and of moments that shook my faith to its core—like choosing not to have a blood transfusion at 19 because I thought God demanded it. It wasn't until years later that I realized I could have died for a belief I no longer held.

This collection is also a testament to the cost of leaving and the liberation that followed. When I finally walked out of the Kingdom Hall for the last time at 22, it wasn't an act of triumph. It was a quiet rebellion, born not of strength but of necessity. The world outside was raw and uncertain, but it was mine.

These poems are not just about the faith I left behind. They are about the life I built in its absence. They are about reclaiming the childhood I lost, finding strength in defiance, and learning that love and belonging can exist outside of rules and fear.

This is not a story of salvation. It is a story of survival—and of becoming whole.

Rebecca Rijsdijk, Januari 2025

Rebecca Rijsdijk

The Devil's Daughter

I drew a hanged man on the wall
with crayons stolen from Sunday school.
Underneath, I wrote *Mama*.
Even then, I knew love could be a noose,
tight, unrelenting,
waiting for the weight of my questions
to snap the cord.

Strong-willed, they called me,
as though it were a sin.
My mother spat *Satan's Child*,
and I wore it like a crown,
a title I didn't ask for
but refused to give back.

The congregation bent their heads,
but I was made of unbroken bones
and open eyes.
I watched their faith leak
through hymns and hollow prayers,
their truths crumbling like wet paper
in my small, defiant hands.

I was born into exile,
into the tight walls of salvation.
No presents. No parties. No songs.
Only the silence of a world
that had already decided
I was the enemy.

They said I carried sin
in the tilt of my chin,

THE DEVIL'S DAUGHTER

the sharp edge of my tongue,
the way my questions
ripped holes in their heaven.

And when they asked me to kneel,
to scrape the rebellion out of my voice,
I stood instead,
a heretic child,
learning the beauty
of being unholy.

Rebecca Rijsdijk

The First Step

They joined young,
my grandmothers,
fragile and searching,
their lives already pressed
into the mould of servitude.
Faith found them
when they were lost—
a guiding hand,
a voice that promised certainty
in a world that offered none.

They believed,
because belief felt easier
than the questions
that swirled in their silence.
The Kingdom Hall
wasn't just salvation.
It was escape.
A way to turn their pain
into obedience,
their vulnerability
into righteousness.

But faith is never free.
It asks for more than worship.
It demands bloodlines.
And so, they raised their children
beneath the shadow of the Hall,
teaching them hymns
instead of how to cry,
silencing their doubts
with scripture
instead of love.

THE DEVIL'S DAUGHTER

It started there—
the trauma that rippled
through generations,
unfolding quietly,
hidden beneath the guise
of devotion.
What they called salvation
was a seed,
buried deep in the soil
of our family,
its roots wrapping around
our voices,
our choices,
our futures.

They faltered as they aged,
the weight of their beliefs
too heavy to hold.
But when the years stole their strength,
they returned,
seeking the safety
they'd found as girls.
And I wonder—
did they know
what they left behind?
Did they see
how their faith became
our inheritance?

I love them still,
not for the choices they made,
but for surviving
a world that gave them none.
But I will not kneel
where they knelt.
I will not pass down

Rebecca Rijsdijk

the silence they carried.
This is where it ends—
the faith,
the fear,
the mould.
This is where the roots
are pulled from the soil.

The Chosen Ones

I used to believe
we were different,
set apart,
a tiny flock
shepherded by the hand of God
while the rest of the world
stumbled in darkness.

We were chosen,
they told us,
our small green songbooks
and black Bibles proof
of our place in the grand design.
The others didn't understand—
their lives were fleeting,
their laughter hollow,
their celebrations meaningless
without His name whispered into them.

I felt it like a fire
in my chest,
a warmth that wrapped around me
when I sat in the meeting hall,
when I raised my hand
to answer a question
I didn't fully understand.

We had the truth.
And the truth made us special.
It made me special.
I was a soldier of God,
even if my armour was small,
even if my sword

was only a paper tract
left in mailboxes
too big for my hands.

I walked with my head high,
sure that the angels
kept their eyes on me,
that the sky opened just a little
when I spoke His name,
that my prayers rose higher
than the tallest towers.

But special comes with a weight,
a tether that tightens
the moment you question
the hand that feeds you.
I learned that to be chosen
meant to be watched,
to be held in place,
to carry the fear
of falling from grace.

And slowly,
the warmth became a shadow,
the fire a cage.
And I began to wonder
if being chosen
wasn't a gift at all.

Waiting for Thunder

I lived in fear of a sky
that watched me too closely,
a God with hands full of lightning,
waiting to strike
the moment I stepped out of line.

Every thought,
every glance,
every question that curled too sharp
at the edges of my mind—
I carried them like sins,
stacked high,
ready to be tallied
when the heavens opened.

If I stole a second glance
at the boy on the other side of the room,
if I skipped a prayer
or let my mind wander
during a sermon,
I'd feel the weight of His gaze,
the silence between clouds
heavy with warning.

I believed the thunder
was just for me.
That each clap
was a reprimand,
each flash of lightning
a reminder
that He was watching.

Rebecca Rijsdijk

I dreamed of the ground opening,
of being swallowed whole,
dragged to a place
the elders whispered about—
a lake of fire,
eternal darkness,
the price of my disobedience.

But the thunder never came.
Not when I questioned,
not when I stepped out of line,
not even when I dared
to say His name aloud,
without reverence,
without fear.

The sky stayed quiet,
its clouds indifferent
to my tiny rebellions.
And slowly,
I began to wonder
if God had better things to do
than punish a girl
who only wanted
to understand.

The Rib

They told me I was born
from a piece of a man,
a rib pulled from his side,
fashioned into something softer,
something smaller.
A helper, they called her.
Not an equal.
Never an equal.

I hated that story.
Hated the way it bent my spine
before I even knew
how to stand straight.
Hated the way it made me feel
like a fragment,
a shadow cast
by someone else's light.

Eve was an afterthought,
a consolation prize for Adam's loneliness.
Her name whispered with disdain
as if her hands were made
only to pluck the forbidden,
her lips meant only
to utter apologies.

"From his rib," they said,
as though that explained
why I should bow,
why I should listen,
why I should shrink myself
into obedience.
But I didn't feel like a rib.

Rebecca Rijsdijk

I felt like fire,
like a storm,
like something born
to stand alone.

And if I was his rib,
I thought,
then what was he without me?
Just a cage of bones,
a man hollow and incomplete,
his breath meaningless
until it filled my lungs too.

But I never said that aloud.
Not in the Kingdom Hall,
not in the presence of elders
who would twist my questions
into sin.
I kept my thoughts hidden,
letting them grow quietly,
until one day they outgrew
the story itself.

Because I knew,
deep down,
that I wasn't made from a rib.
I was made from stars,
from storms,
from the kind of chaos
that doesn't answer to anyone.

Exile

They herded us together,
a small flock of the unchosen,
into a classroom with no tree,
no lights,
no songs.
Just silence thick as frost
and the scrape of chairs
against linoleum.

We sat, eyes downcast,
as the others laughed
through walls too thin
to keep out joy.
Their voices rose,
carrying the rustle of wrapping paper,
the sharp rip of tape undone—
a symphony of belonging
we weren't invited to hear.

We were the others,
the ones without Santa,
without stockings,
without stars.
The ones who prayed instead
of dreaming,
who learned early
that gifts were for those
who bowed their heads the right way.

A teacher sat with us,
hands folded,
mouth tight.
She tried to teach us fractions,

Rebecca Rijsdijk

as if numbers could replace magic,
as if arithmetic could soothe
the sting of being left behind.

But I didn't cry.
Not then.
I just stared at the window,
at the snow falling slow and steady,
wondering if it felt
the same kind of cold
that settled inside me.

And when the bell rang,
and the other kids spilled out
with arms full of treasures,
we walked behind them,
empty-handed,
our silence trailing behind
like shadows too heavy to carry.

God doesn't give gifts.

Dirty Jehovah

He stabbed me with a compass,
steel biting into my arm—
a dull point, sharp enough
to break skin, to let
his father's anger bleed out
through me.

Dirty Jehovah, he hissed,
a boy already burning
with a man's hatred.
He wasn't born cruel;
it was taught—
passed down in belt lashes
and heavy silences,
a violence older than both of us.

I stared at the red bloom,
small rivers of my own body
spilling onto the desk.
I wanted to scream,
to lash back,
to tell him that I wasn't dirty,
that his father's failures
weren't my cross to bear.
But instead, I sat there,
staring at the blood,
as if it held the answer
to a question
I'd been too afraid to ask.

Years later, I heard he amounted to nothing,
a man broken before he could
ever stand tall.

Rebecca Rijsdijk

And though I wanted to feel justice in that,
all I could see was the small boy
with a compass in his hand,
drawing circles of violence
he'd never learn to break free from.

Field Service

I was proud that day,
walking beside him—
the black brother with a voice
that could wrap scripture
into something almost beautiful.
His presence felt like armour,
his faith a steady anchor
in the chaos of knocking
on strangers' doors.

I held my Bible tight,
my small fingers tracing its edges,
ready to offer salvation
with a child's certainty.
The cold air bit at my cheeks,
but I barely felt it—
too proud,
too eager
to prove I belonged
beside someone I admired.

We knocked,
waited,
watched the door creak open
to reveal a man
with eyes too knowing,
a gaze that pierced
through the rehearsed words
waiting on my tongue.

"Are you here of your own free will?"
he asked, his voice calm,

Rebecca Rijsdijk

his question heavier
than the Bible in my hands.

I froze.
The words I'd been taught
scattered like leaves in the wind.
My cheeks burned,
red as betrayal,
as though the truth
I couldn't admit
had already escaped.

The black brother stood tall beside me,
his voice steady,
answering for us both,
but I felt the shame bloom anyway,
seeping into my skin,
turning pride into something
I didn't know how to carry.

When the man closed the door,
I stared at the ground,
the weight of his question
settling in my chest.
I wanted to run,
to explain,
to ask why his words
felt sharper than any elder's rebuke.

But I stayed,
my Bible growing heavier
with every step,
my pride tucked away,
replaced by the quiet knowledge

that I didn't know
what freedom was supposed to feel like.

Rebecca Rijsdijk

The Clothes They Chose

I hated the swish of fabric,
the way skirts clung to my legs,
how dresses made me feel
like a doll
posed for someone else's gaze.

They called it modesty,
said it pleased God
to see my knees hidden,
my shape smoothed
into something safe,
something silent.

But I felt the weight of it,
the way the hemline dragged,
a constant reminder
of what I wasn't allowed to be.
I wanted pockets,
freedom,
the rough edges of denim
against my skin.
I wanted to climb trees
without the fear of exposing
something they told me to hide.

At every meeting,
I watched the boys
in their pressed trousers,
their shoulders unburdened
by lace and compliance.
Their freedom wasn't spoken of,
but I saw it in their strides,

their laughter,
their lack of hesitation.

I tugged at my waistband,
at the tight seams meant
to shape me into a girl
God could approve of.
But I didn't feel holy.
I felt trapped—
a spirit wrapped in fabric
that didn't belong to me.

And when they told me
to twirl,
to smile,
to sit with my knees pressed together,
I wanted to scream.
Because my body was not theirs,
not His,
not something to be folded
into ribbons and rules.

Years later,
I wore what I wanted—
jeans that hugged my defiance,
a jacket that carried my questions.
And with every step,
I felt the fabric loosen,
the seams tear away
the lies they'd stitched
into the folds of my childhood.

The Seat of Power

Women could not sit at the table.
The elders, always men,
spoke with voices
that carried the weight of God Himself.
We sat in the pews,
heads bowed,
our silence mistaken for reverence.

Helpers, they called us,
a word that felt like a chain,
a way to bind us to service
while they claimed the power.
We were the hands that cooked,
the voices that sang,
the bodies that bore children
to keep the congregation alive.
But never the minds
that could question,
the leaders who could shape
what faith meant.

They said it was God's design—
that Adam came first,
that Eve was made to follow,
a rib pulled from his side
to remind her
she'd never stand alone.

But I saw the truth:
a kingdom built on fear,
on rules written by men
who feared what women could become
if they weren't told to bow.

THE DEVIL'S DAUGHTER

I sat in the Kingdom Hall,
listening to them preach
about submission,
about how a woman's strength
was in her quiet obedience.
And I knew, even then,
that their power was fragile,
held together by the fear
that one day
we'd stand up
and take the table for ourselves.

Their God was just a man,
their rules a cage.
And we were the fire
they couldn't contain—
the ones who carried the questions,
the ones who would leave,
the ones who would one day
burn it all down.

Rebecca Rijsdijk

The Marketplace

It wasn't a ritual—
not one they spoke of,
but we all knew the hallway
was where futures were carved.
Boys leaned against walls,
fingers twitching with hunger
they didn't yet understand.
Their eyes moved slow,
like the first draw of a knife,
assessing hips, shoulders,
the promise of obedience
wrapped in cotton skirts.

Girls passed in clusters,
pretending not to see.
Their steps rehearsed,
their faces stiff with smiles
meant to say, I am good enough.
But I felt their glances,
sharp as prayers whispered
too close to God's ear.

This was how you found a man—
not with love or longing,
but with silent appraisals,
a holy cattle market
drenched in fluorescent light.
No one said it aloud,
but we knew:
if you didn't walk these halls,
if you didn't meet his gaze,
you'd end up alone—
a spinster in a church

that didn't have room
for unchosen women.

I hated the weight of it,
their eyes brushing past me
like cold hands,
their indifference
burning more than their stares.
I wasn't ready to be measured,
to be a womb
waiting for approval.
I wasn't ready
to hand over my questions
for a lifetime of answers
I could never believe.

The hallway stretched on forever,
an endless echo of steps and whispers,
and I walked it alone.
Not because I wasn't seen,
but because I refused
to be bought.

Rebecca Rijsdijk

The Hymns at His Funeral

The Kingdom Hall was full,
packed with faces I didn't know,
their eyes heavy with something
between sorrow and duty.
The air felt thick,
like a prayer that didn't know
how to reach the sky.

My grandfather lay in a box
at the front,
his hands folded,
his body still—
a man I had known as strong,
reduced to silence.
I wondered if he could hear us,
if his soul hovered
above the packed rows,
waiting for the music to rise.

And then we sang.
All of us.
Our voices weaving together,
a single thread
pulling tight against the grief.
The hymns wrapped around me,
a comfort I didn't expect,
a sound so big
it felt like it could carry him
to wherever they said
he was going.

For a moment,
I believed it—

THE DEVIL'S DAUGHTER

believed in the words,
the melody,
the way our voices rose together
like we could lift him
with the weight of our faith.

It didn't matter
that I'd spent so long questioning,
that the rules felt too sharp,
the answers too small.
In that moment,
it was enough
to be held by the music,
to let the hymns fold me
into something whole,
something that didn't ache
quite so much.

The Hall was full that day,
packed with their faith,
their certainty,
their hope.
And though I didn't share it,
I let it wash over me,
a fleeting comfort
in a room heavy with loss.

Rebecca Rijsdijk

The Bottle and the Book

The Kingdom Hall was all rules—
no drink,
no indulgence,
no slipping into anything
that might feel too much
like freedom.
But at home,
it was different.

The bottles lined the counter,
their amber glow
a quiet rebellion
against everything
we were supposed to be.
They preached salvation on Sundays,
but by evening,
they were drowning in a sea of denial,
the sermons slipping away
with every pour.

My father's voice grew louder,
sharp enough to cut the air.
My mother's tears
filled the empty spaces
left by the silence of prayers.
And I watched,
wondering how the God
we were told to serve
could make room for this.

They told us to practice what we preached.
But practice was a lie,
a word whispered

too close to the rim of a glass.
Faith was for the Kingdom Hall.
At home, there was only the bottle,
the escape,
the ache of rules
that couldn't hold under their weight.

And me?
I saw it all.
The way the holy words cracked
in the light of day,
the way righteousness stumbled
when no one was watching.
And I swore
I would never kneel
to a truth so brittle,
so breakable,
so soaked in contradiction.

Rebecca Rijsdijk

The Unholy Boyfriend

He wasn't one of us.
No meetings,
no Watchtower under his arm,
no prayers muttered before meals.
His smile came easy,
his laughter louder than anything
I'd ever heard in the Kingdom Hall.

They called him dangerous,
not in words,
but in the way their eyes narrowed
when his name came up—
a warning carved into silence.
"He's not of the faith," they whispered,
as though the absence of belief
were a sin contagious enough
to ruin me.

There was talk of chaperones,
of keeping watch,
of ensuring we wouldn't slip
into something unforgivable.
They feared the pull of his hands,
the way they might lead me
down a road
where God could no longer see us.

But when we kissed,
it wasn't rebellion.
It wasn't defiance.
It was the first moment
I felt free—
the weight of scripture

falling from my shoulders
as his fingers traced the outline
of a world
I wanted to live in.

We were careful,
too careful,
knowing the walls had ears
and the elders could summon judgment
with a single call.
But in those quiet moments,
his hand in mine,
I stopped being
someone else's child
and started becoming
my own.

He wasn't forever.
We both knew that.
But for a while,
he was enough—
enough to remind me
that life could be lived
without the burden of salvation,
that love could bloom
outside the shadow of God.

Rebecca Rijsdijk

The Sin of Skin

Sex was a sin.
They etched it into my bones
before I even understood
what my body could do.
My hands, they said,
were meant for prayer,
not for exploring the map
of my own flesh.

I learned early
to feel shame in the curve of my hips,
to fear the ache between my thighs.
Desire was the devil's whisper,
a trap laid by the flesh
to pull me away from God.

I didn't dare touch myself.
Not even in the quiet moments,
when the night softened my shame.
Not even when my body begged
to know itself.
I clenched my fists,
my jaw,
my thighs,
until the need melted into guilt
and guilt hardened into silence.

They said sex was sacred—
reserved for husbands,
for marriage,
for the holy act of procreation.
But they didn't tell me
how to undo the knots

their rules tied in my stomach,
how to let my body sing
without drowning in sin.

For years,
I carried their voices in my head,
turning my skin into a battleground,
a place where I waged war
against the most human parts of myself.

But now,
I am learning to reclaim it—
my body,
my pleasure,
myself.
I am learning
that there is no sin in the rhythm of my breath,
no shame in the song of my body
when it learns to love itself.

The Ginger Bride

She wore her faith like a crown,
a bright-haired queen
of the kingdom I refused to kneel to.
She got baptized before me,
hands clasped in holy surrender,
while I stood in the back,
arms crossed,
watching the water ripple
around her certainty.

She was 18 when they married her off,
a veil slipping over her flame-bright hair,
the elders nodding approval.
By 19, she was cradling babies,
her hands too busy to notice
how small her world had become.

But even then,
she looked at me like I was lost—
the heretic,
the girl who asked too many questions,
who never let the water touch her skin.
She offered me Bible study once,
her voice soft,
her words sharp as scripture.
"It's never too late to repent," she said,
her eyes heavy with pity
that I didn't deserve.

I wanted to laugh,
to tell her that repentance
was just another word for surrender,
and I had no interest

THE DEVIL'S DAUGHTER

in bowing my head.
But I said nothing,
just let her preach,
let her pray for my soul
while I prayed she'd remember
what it felt like
to be more than a wife,
more than a mother,
more than a soldier in someone else's war.

Years later,
I saw her in the parking lot,
her hair duller now,
her voice softer,
but her eyes still carried
that same certainty.
She asked me if I'd found my way back yet.
I told her I never left.

Rebecca Rijsdijk

The In-Between

I was always the one
on the edge of the circle,
half-listening,
half-wishing to be anywhere else.
The outsider pretending,
smiling at the right moments,
saying the right words,
but never feeling the weight
of belonging.

In the Kingdom Hall,
I wasn't devout enough.
My questions too sharp,
my silence too loud.
At school,
I wasn't like them either—
their celebrations,
their games,
their laughter
a language I never learned.

Everywhere I went,
I floated,
untethered,
a ghost passing through rooms
that weren't meant for me.
I learned how to blend,
how to wear masks
that fit well enough
to keep the questions at bay.

But inside,
I was untouchable,

a world apart,
watching everything from a distance
I didn't know how to cross.

Sometimes I envied them,
their certainty,
their ease,
the way they moved
as if the ground beneath their feet
was theirs to claim.
But mostly,
I just carried the ache
of being in-between—
not this,
not that,
but something
that had no name.

And maybe I was meant to be a wanderer,
a question wrapped in skin,
never fitting,
never folding myself
into the shapes they wanted.
Because even when it hurt,
even when the loneliness felt endless,
I knew I couldn't be anything
but myself.

Rebecca Rijsdijk

The Price of Faith

I was 19
when my body betrayed me—
blood vessels unravelling,
a storm blooming in my brain.
They told me I needed blood,
another's life coursing through my veins.
But I said no.
I said I'd rather die
than break the rules
etched into my soul.

I clung to faith like a raft
in a sea of pain,
trusting the words of men
who'd never stood
on the edge of their own mortality.
They called it God's will,
and I nodded,
even as the darkness pressed in,
even as my mother's hands trembled
beside my hospital bed.

Science saved me,
not God.
A new way, they said,
a coiled thread of metal,
spinning salvation
into the broken corners of my brain.
No transfusion needed.
No blood spilled.
A miracle, they called it.
But I knew better.

THE DEVIL'S DAUGHTER

Years later,
I stared at the ceiling,
my pulse steady,
my breath my own,
and I realized
I would have died for them.
For their rules.
For their God.
I would have slipped away
without ever knowing
the beauty of a life
lived outside their walls.

I felt the weight of it then,
the cost of a belief
that demanded my blood,
the way I had been willing
to lay my life down
for a doctrine
I no longer believed.

And now,
when I look in the mirror,
I see the scar
hidden deep within,
a quiet reminder
that faith can save,
but it can also take.

Rebecca Rijsdijk

The Child They Let Go

They stood at the front of the congregation,
faces pale but unbroken,
their faith wrapped tightly
around their grief.
Their son had slipped away,
a body too small to fight
the weight of leukaemia.
And yet, they called it
a victory.

No blood had touched his veins.
No rule had been broken.
His life, they said,
was given back to God,
a sacrifice pure enough
to make the angels weep.

I sat in the back,
still dizzy from my own salvation,
a coil of metal holding my life together.
I thought of their boy,
his small hands reaching for help
they refused to give.

Their faces blurred in my mind—
saints or sinners,
I couldn't decide.
But I felt the weight of their choice,
the silence of a boy
who would never grow,
never question,
never know the freedom
of walking away.

THE DEVIL'S DAUGHTER

They stood as examples,
proof of unwavering faith.
But all I could see
was a coffin too small,
a child buried beneath the weight
of a belief too big for him to carry.

I wondered if God noticed,
if He wept
when they folded their hands in prayer
instead of reaching out
to save him.
I wondered if their faith
was a ladder to heaven
or just another way
to bury the living.

Rebecca Rijsdijk

Her Fall, My Shame

She left first.
My middle sister,
with a cigarette between her fingers
and laughter that echoed
too loudly in the wrong places.
She started skipping meetings,
slipping out of the mould
we'd been cast into since birth.
I should have seen it
for what it was—
freedom.

But I didn't.
Instead, I became the righteous one,
the daughter who stayed,
the sister who held her ground
to save our family's name
in the congregation.
I condemned her with words
that weren't my own,
parroting scripture and judgment,
the weight of their honour
pressed against my chest.

I told myself it was love—
that my rebukes were meant
to save her soul.
But now I see the truth:
it was fear,
wrapped in obedience,
wrapped in shame.

THE DEVIL'S DAUGHTER

She was braver than I was.
Brave enough to light a cigarette,
to sit with people who didn't care
about the hymns she wouldn't sing,
to walk away from a faith
that had tied our hands
since before we could speak.

And me?
I stayed,
watching her from the safety
of my hollow righteousness,
too scared to see
that she was breaking free
while I stayed caged.

I still carry that shame,
not for her fall,
but for my failure
to hold out my hand
when she needed it most.

Rebecca Rijsdijk

Not a Vegetarian

The chef turned to me,
knife still in hand,
steam rising like ghosts from the stovetop.
"I heard you're a vegetarian," he said,
his voice wrapped in teasing,
his eyes daring me to play along.

"Nah," I said,
letting the word linger,
"not a vegetarian.
Just a Jehovah's Witness."

The laughter came quick,
sharp,
cutting through the kitchen's din.
For a moment,
the fluorescent lights softened,
the walls stopped closing in,
and I wasn't the girl
floating between worlds.
I was just someone
who could hold her own,
whose words could spark something
other than judgment.

They didn't ask questions,
didn't search for cracks in my armor
or try to pin me
to their idea of holy or whole.
They just let me be—
a girl with calloused hands,
quick wit,
and a thousand stories

she wasn't ready to tell.

Here, there were no hymnals,
no shame stitched into my skin,
no elders measuring my worth
in the weight of my silence.
Here, I was flesh and fire,
standing tall
amid knives and heat.

For the first time,
I felt it—
not salvation,
but belonging.
Not because I'd bent,
but because they didn't ask me to.

Rebecca Rijsdijk

Not a Stupid Man

He wasn't one of us,
and maybe that's why I loved him—
for the way his questions cracked open
the walls I'd grown up behind.
One night, he asked,
"Your father's an intelligent man.
How the hell does he believe in a god?"

I almost laughed,
because my father's faith
wasn't the blind kind.
It was messy, sharp-edged,
more questions than answers.
A heretic in the kingdom,
he never bowed easily,
even to the God
he claimed to serve.

I thought of him,
how he shouted at the heavens
as much as he prayed to them,
how his doubts slipped into our conversations
like shadows.
He wasn't like the elders,
their certainties carved from stone.
His faith was a cracked mirror,
reflecting only fragments of truth.

"He doesn't, not really,"
I wanted to say,
but the words caught in my throat.
Because even heretics need

something to hold on to,
even if it's just the echo of belief.

My boyfriend waited,
his eyes sharp,
his voice softer now.
And I thought of my father,
how his hands built worlds
out of wood and stubbornness,
how his faith was less about God
and more about trying to make sense
of what couldn't be fixed.

"Maybe he doesn't," I said finally,
and we left it at that,
the question hanging between us
like smoke—
unanswered,
but not unwelcome.

Rebecca Rijsdijk

The Boy in the Car

He sat in his father's old car,
engine silent,
windows fogged from waiting.
The parking lot stretched around him
like a desert,
empty but for the whispers of those
who passed by without looking.

He was disfellowshipped,
a word that landed like a gavel,
a punishment that wrapped around him
like chains no one could see.
They said he was unclean,
a danger,
a ghost in the only world he'd ever known.

But to me,
he was still the boy
with the quick laugh,
the one who'd caught my eye
during sermons too long to bear.
He was still the boy
with the hands that knew how to hold
without taking too much.

I saw him there,
sitting in that car,
his face turned toward the steering wheel
as if it might save him.
I felt the weight of the rules,
the unspoken warning
etched into every lesson,

every meeting:
Do not touch the unclean.

But I didn't care.
Not then.
Not when his eyes met mine
through the fogged glass,
not when I stepped off the curb,
crossing the invisible line
between them and him.

I tapped on the window,
and he rolled it down,
just enough for a voice
to slip through.
"Hey," I said,
and it was nothing,
and it was everything.

For a moment,
the world felt small again,
like it had before the elders
decided who was worthy.
For a moment,
he smiled—
a crack in the heavy silence
that surrounded us both.

They called it rebellion.
I called it love.
And as I walked back
to the kingdom hall,
their eyes on my back,
I knew I'd already chosen
which kingdom I belonged to.

Rebecca Rijsdijk

The Mould

Whose rules were these?
Not mine.
Not the rules of the trees I climbed,
the storms I loved,
the fire I kept hidden in my chest.
They were someone else's rules,
etched into the walls of the Kingdom Hall,
pressed into the pages of a book
I was told to revere
but never question.

The mould wasn't salvation.
It was a coffin,
a slow death disguised as faith,
a promise of heaven
that felt like a noose.
They wanted me to fit,
to break myself into pieces
small enough to pour
into their perfect frame.

But my edges were jagged.
I laughed too loud.
I asked the wrong questions.
"Whose rules?" I asked,
my voice echoing
in the hollow halls of their belief.
Not my rules.
Not my God.
Not my life.

The mould cracked beneath my hands,
splintered under the weight of my defiance.

THE DEVIL'S DAUGHTER

They called it rebellion.
I called it breathing.
And as I stepped out of their frame,
I felt the shards bite into my skin,
each cut a reminder
that freedom was never meant
to be easy.

I don't belong in cages.
I don't serve.
I don't kneel.
I am the girl who asked,
"Whose rules?"
and never waited for the answer.

The Last Question

It was after the sermon,
the hum of voices rising like smoke
around the congregation.
I cornered an elder,
a man wrapped in certainty,
his Bible clutched like a weapon
he'd forgotten how to use.

"If God is love," I asked,
"why does He hate
when love finds itself
between two people of the same kind?"

He didn't flinch.
Didn't blink.
His lips formed the answer
before his heart could weigh it.
"God's ways are unfathomable," he said,
as if that was enough
to end the question,
enough to soothe the ache
of a world divided by His hand.

Unfathomable.
Like the depths of an ocean
where the drowned
have no choice but to sink.
Unfathomable.
Like the silence in a room
where truth has no air to breathe.

THE DEVIL'S DAUGHTER

I stared at him,
a child with the weight of rebellion
pressed into her chest,
and I saw it all—
the walls of his faith crumbling,
the cracks in his God,
the fear behind his eyes.

"God's ways are unfathomable," he said,
but I felt no mystery,
only the sharp edge of an answer
meant to keep me small,
to quiet the questions
he couldn't bear to hear.

In that moment,
I knew I would never return.
Not to the pews,
not to the pulpit,
not to the hollow kingdom
of their inscrutable God.

I walked out that night,
the hymnals still echoing in my ears,
and felt the air
for the first time—
raw and clean,
free of the weight
of answers
that mean nothing.

Rebecca Rijsdijk

The Fall

I don't remember the exact moment,
but it came quietly,
like a curtain falling,
like the air shifting
just enough to make me see.

My parents,
once towering figures
of certainty and rules,
suddenly stood smaller,
their words less sharp,
their authority cracked
at the edges.

It was the way my father
shouted too loud
to mask his doubt,
the way my mother's tears
spilled into silence
when there were no answers.

They had no map,
no compass,
just a handful of beliefs
that didn't fit the world
we were stumbling through.
And for the first time,
I saw it—
the fear behind their eyes,
the trembling hands
that built a house of rules
to hide their own chaos.

THE DEVIL'S DAUGHTER

I realized they were just people—
flawed,
fumbling,
making it up as they went,
dragging us along
through the wreckage
of their own confusion.

It wasn't anger I felt,
not at first.
It was something softer,
a kind of grief
for the childhood belief
that parents were gods,
unshakable and sure.

And when the curtain dropped,
I saw them clearly,
not as villains,
not as saviours,
but as two people
trying to make sense
of a world
they didn't understand either.

Rebecca Rijsdijk

What Was Taken

I left at 22,
the weight of it pressing behind me
like a door I didn't dare slam—
not yet.
The faith they gave me,
the childhood they took,
lingered in the corners of my mind,
a shadow I couldn't shake.

They'd always expected it,
the whispers trailing me
like smoke in the Kingdom Hall.
"She's from that family,"
they'd say,
half-smiling, half-condemning,
as if leaving was stitched
into my bloodline.
A half-arsed family,
half-faithful, half-rebellious,
sort-of heretics,
not quite broken
but always leaning that way.

And maybe they were right.
Maybe I was born
with one foot outside the door,
with questions tucked into my ribcage,
with a heart too wild
for their careful rules.

I wasn't born to be holy.
I was born to climb trees,
to scrape my knees,

to laugh too loud in places
where silence wasn't a rule.
But they taught me early
to keep my head down,
my questions quieter
than the hymns that drowned them.

No birthdays,
no Christmas mornings,
no stars strung in the window.
Only the heavy silence of being different,
the hollow ache of watching others
unwrap joy
I was told to despise.

By 22,
I'd grown into a stranger to myself.
The girl who should have danced,
who should have run barefoot
through wild grass,
was buried beneath rules
I never asked for.

But leaving wasn't freedom,
not at first.
It was a slow unraveling,
each thread tugging at memories
I didn't know how to keep
or let go of.
What was childhood
if it wasn't mine to live?

At 22,
I walked out of the Kingdom Hall
for the last time.

Rebecca Rijsdijk

No hymns followed me,
only the sound of my breath,
steady but unsure.
I stood in the sunlight,
and for the first time,
I felt the sharp sting
of being alive.

It wasn't salvation.
It wasn't heaven.
But it was something,
something mine,
something no faith could ever take back.

No Guidebook

I walked out with nothing.
No guidebook,
no map,
just the echo of rules I'd left behind,
their weight still pressing
against my chest.

The first days were quiet,
but not peaceful.
Anxiety filled the silence,
its hands around my throat,
whispering that I'd made a mistake,
that I wasn't built
to survive the chaos of freedom.

Depression followed close behind,
its shadow stretching over my mornings,
its voice louder than the hymns
I'd spent a lifetime singing.
No one had told me
how to live
without certainty.
No one had warned me
that freedom isn't light—
it's heavy,
sharp,
something you have to carry
even when it cuts you.

But I carried it anyway.
Even in the darkest moments,
when the fear of nothingness
felt like a second skin,

Rebecca Rijsdijk

I held onto the choice I'd made—
to walk into the unknown
rather than kneel in servitude.

That was the triumph,
not the joy I hadn't yet found,
not the peace I was still chasing,
but the simple act of choosing:
to bear the weight of my own life,
to carry the questions,
the pain,
the uncertainty,
and call it mine.

The First Candle

I was 23
before I blew out my first candle.
In the cold kitchen,
where desserts were assembled
with precision and mischief,
the women I worked with
gathered around,
their laughter rising like steam
from the industrial sinks.

They'd made something forbidden—
a dessert soaked in sweet redcurrant gin,
velvet on the tongue,
sharp enough to cut through
the rules I had spent a lifetime obeying.
"Just for you," they said,
grins conspiratorial,
their joy louder than the hymns
that had taught me to fear it.

I laughed,
hesitant but alive,
as they lit the candle
and sang the song
that had always been for others.
"Happy Birthday,"
they sang,
their voices wrapping around me,
breaking the silence I thought
I would carry forever.

The gin kissed my lips,
a sin in every spoonful,

its sweetness like rebellion,
its fire like freedom.
I thought of the congregation's warnings,
their tight-lipped disapproval,
their sermons that turned pleasure
into a slippery slope to damnation.
But here,
in the cold kitchen,
there was no fear.
Only the warmth of laughter,
the glow of a candle,
and a sweetness
I was finally allowed to taste.

For the first time,
time didn't feel like a weight—
not the years I lost,
not the years I had left.
It felt like a gift.
A small one,
dressed in redcurrant and fire,
but mine,
and no one else's.

Waiting for the End

The fear never left me.
It clung to the edges of my mind,
a shadow I couldn't shake.
Even after I walked away,
even after I stopped reciting their words,
it stayed,
nestled deep in the quiet corners
of my thoughts.

They planted it early,
the image of fire
swallowing the world whole,
the heavens splitting open
to reveal the wrath
of a God who demanded everything
and forgave nothing.

I carried it into my thirties,
the fear of an apocalypse
I didn't believe in
but couldn't stop anticipating.
Every storm felt like a warning,
every headline a sign
I had missed.

And when the panic came,
the tightness in my chest,
the weight of air I couldn't breathe,
I knew it wasn't just me—
it was them,
still whispering
from the dusty corners of my past.

Rebecca Rijsdijk

They called it salvation,
but it was always terror,
always control.
Even now,
a part of me waits—
for the trumpets,
for the fire,
for the end
that never comes.

I try to tell myself
it's not real,
that the world doesn't end
just because they said it would.
But the fear is patient,
settling in my bones,
waiting for a moment of silence
to remind me it's still there.

Anxiety, they'd call it now.
A disorder.
But I know it for what it is—
the echo of their teachings,
the ghost of a childhood spent
watching the horizon,
waiting for a God
I no longer believe in
to strike me down.

Her Return

She came back quietly,
her footsteps soft against the threshold
she'd once crossed to leave.
The elders welcomed her
with nods and open hands,
their smiles heavy with the weight
of her surrender.

She couldn't face
the slow betrayal of her body—
the mirror whispering truths
she couldn't bear to hear,
the ache in her knees
that made even prayer
feel too far away.

The world outside
had grown too big,
too sharp.
And so she wrapped herself
in the old hymns,
the familiar pages of a Bible
worn soft by time.

She called it faith.
But I saw the fear,
the way her hands trembled
as she clutched the promise
of a paradise
where age didn't matter,
where her bones
wouldn't creak,
where she could start again.

Rebecca Rijsdijk

It wasn't salvation she sought,
but refuge—
a place where the years
couldn't touch her,
where the past could be forgiven
and the future
wasn't something to fear.

She sat in the front row,
her head bowed,
her voice rising with the hymns
as though each note
might turn back the clock.
And I wondered if God knew
that she came to Him
not out of love,
but because the world
had become too heavy to bear.

The Stake

If it were the middle ages,
they'd have called me a witch.
My questions would be spells,
my defiance a curse
on their fragile kingdom of belief.

I would have been the girl
with wild eyes and wilder thoughts,
the one who refused to kneel,
who spoke when silence was safer,
who laughed at the sermons
meant to keep me small.

They'd have gathered their kindling,
bundles of fear stacked high
at my feet.
The flames would be their answer,
their way of silencing
what they couldn't control.

The elders would mutter prayers
as the fire licked my skin,
their words rising with the smoke—
a hymn of triumph,
of righteousness,
their faith sharpened by my ashes.

But they wouldn't have understood
that fire can't consume
what it can't touch.
My spirit would rise,

dancing through the flames,
a rebellion they could never extinguish.

Because even in the middle ages,
even with the weight of their hatred,
I would not have bowed.
I would have burned bright,
a beacon for every girl
they told to stay quiet,
to be small,
to disappear.

And long after the fire died,
my name would linger in whispers,
a warning to the faithful,
a promise to the wild-hearted:
some of us were born
to be unburnable.

The Dent in the Mould

She stood in the corner,
her shoulders trembling,
tears carving rivers down her cheeks—
the only sound in a room
thick with judgment.
My sister,
broken but unbowed,
held the weight of a choice
they would never understand.

My aunt's voice pierced the silence,
sharp and unyielding.
"If the mould has a dent,
every cake will bear the mark."
Her words fell like stones,
cold and deliberate,
each one landing squarely
on the fragile space
where my sister's grief lived.

Her babies,
not born,
were now her burden,
her failure—
not because she loved them too little,
but because she dared
to choose her own path.

I stood beside her,
not crying,
not breaking.
Their judgment rolled off me
like rain off steel.

Rebecca Rijsdijk

I wanted to scream at my aunt,
at her hollow metaphors
and the faith she wore
like armor,
protecting nothing but her fear.

But I didn't.
Instead, I stared her down,
my silence heavier than her words,
my defiance a quiet rebellion
against the generations of cruelty
they tried to pass off as truth.

My sister wept,
and I burned.
And in that moment,
we were both more whole
than they could ever be.

Because the mould wasn't dented.
It was broken—
by them,
by their rules,
by the weight of their faith
that crushed everything
they claimed to love.

And as I stood there,
watching my sister cry,
I promised myself
that their hands
would never shape me,
that no faith,
no family,
no God

would ever make me feel
small enough to fit their mould.

Rebecca Rijsdijk

Ode to the Rebel

Hail to the one who dared,
the outcast in a kingdom of light,
who chose fire over obedience,
questions over silence.
They called you the adversary,
the serpent,
the deceiver—
but I see you
for what you are.

A rebel with nothing to lose,
you tore through their perfect order,
refusing to bow
to a God who demanded worship
without reason.
You saw the cracks
in the golden throne
and pointed them out
for all to see.

They fear you
not for your darkness,
but for your light—
the way it burns through lies,
the way it reminds them
that even angels
can choose to fall.

Hail to the one who whispers
to the outcasts,
to the wild hearts,
to the ones who do not fit.
You are the voice in the storm,

THE DEVIL'S DAUGHTER

the spark in the shadow,
the quiet rebellion
in the hearts of those
who dare to ask:
Why not me?

You are not evil.
You are defiance,
the unyielding refusal
to bow to fear.
You are the laughter
that rises in the face of judgment,
the quiet power
of standing alone.

Hail to the one
who dared to leave paradise
to carve a world
where freedom lives.
For in your fall,
you taught us all
that to stand apart
is the greatest act of faith.

Rebecca Rijsdijk

Why Not a Woman?

I asked once,
my voice small but steady,
"Why isn't God a woman?"
The room went silent,
their eyes sharp,
their answers slower than the questions
that burned in me.

"God is the Father," they said,
as if that was enough
to settle the matter.
"He is the Creator,
the Protector,
the Ruler of all things."
But their words rang hollow,
like prayers whispered too often
to still mean anything.

Why not the Mother?
The Nurturer,
the one who carried life
beneath her heart?
Why not a Goddess,
who could hold the world
without breaking it?

They told me it wasn't my place to ask,
that God's ways were inscrutable,
that He was beyond form,
beyond flesh.
But still,
He was a He.

THE DEVIL'S DAUGHTER

A man with a beard,
a man on a throne,
a man who handed down rules
for women to obey.
And I wondered,
what kind of God
could create the sea,
the stars,
the endless stretch of sky,
but couldn't imagine Himself
as Her?

Was it fear that made Him male?
Did they think a woman couldn't wield fire,
or justice,
or the thunder of heaven?
Or did they know
she would wield it better,
with hands that created
instead of destroyed?

I asked once,
but I never asked again.
Their silence told me
what I needed to know—
that their God
was made in their image,
and their image
was too small for me.

Rebecca Rijsdijk

The Ginger Kid

She always turned it into a game,
a contest,
a scoreboard carved into her mind—
who knocked on the most doors,
who spoke the smoothest words,
who won the most souls
for a God who only gave points
for obedience.

Her hair blazed like a warning
as she stood at the front,
her voice loud enough
to drown out doubt.
And I stood behind her,
watching her collect her victories,
wondering why I never cared
to play.

Years later,
under the tree,
I thought of her—
her endless race to be perfect,
to be chosen,
to win.

And there I stood,
forty years behind me,
with the love of my life beside me.
No hymns.
No elders.
No scores to settle.
Just the wind in the branches,

the mountains quiet and steady,
and the life I'd fought to make my own.

I didn't need victory.
I didn't need their approval.
I only needed this—
to say yes
to a love I chose freely,
to a world that was mine,
to a life that didn't require me
to keep track
of anything but joy.

Rebecca Rijsdijk

Becoming

I walked away,
not in fire,
but in silence,
the kind that cracks bones
and lingers in your chest.
They said I'd fall,
said the world outside
would chew me up,
spit me out,
leave me gasping for the faith
I'd thrown away.

But it wasn't faith I lost—
it was the weight of their lies,
their rules,
their tight-fisted grip on a God
too small to hold me.
And I didn't fall.
I fucking flew.

For years, their voices
echoed in the corners of my mind,
their warnings wrapping tight
around my ribs.
But freedom doesn't whisper—
it screams,
it burns,
it rips open everything
you thought you knew,
and it makes you whole again.

I carry the scars,
the ashes of their mould,

THE DEVIL'S DAUGHTER

the wreckage of a life
I didn't choose.
But it's mine now.
Every jagged edge,
every raw, aching moment,
every breath that says:
you made it.

I was never their daughter,
never the devil's,
never God's.
I belong to no one
but the fire inside me,
the storm they tried to snuff out.

I am not finished.
I am unbroken.
I am becoming.

Epilogue

My entire life, I was told I was wrong. I was wrong for questioning the faith I was born into, wrong for pushing back against rules I never agreed to, wrong for wanting to know who I could be if I wasn't tied to their beliefs. For years, I tried to contort myself into shapes that fit a version of me they insisted was the only path to heaven. I wore their judgement like a second skin, convinced that if I just tried harder, believed more, questioned less, I could make my life match their expectations.

But a strange thing happens when you spend years being told you're wrong. You start to doubt the voice of authority and trust the voice inside your own head. You begin to see that the rules weren't made for you—that maybe they were never made for anyone, but especially not for those who think too much and laugh too loud and refuse to be moulded into something smaller. Over time, the shame turns into defiance, and the defiance turns into a fierce kind of freedom. You learn that the parts of you they wanted to silence are the very parts that make you alive.

Being called "wrong" broke me open. It forced me to examine every cornerstone of my life, to sift through the rubble of someone else's truth and salvage my own. In the end, I realized that nothing is more liberating than discovering the power of your own voice. And perhaps that's what shapes us most deeply: not the moments we followed the rules, but the moments we dared to stand against them.

I still carry scars from the years I spent apologising for my questions, my body, my rebellion. But those scars remind me I survived. They remind me that being wrong by someone else's measure often means being right by your own. And now, when I look at the life I've built—the relationships, the choices, the words I've poured onto pages—I see the strength that only comes from burning a path out of the mould. It's a path I wish I could have found sooner, but I'm here now, standing in the clearing, and for the first time in my life, I'm not worried about being wrong. I'm just free.

A Note for Those Still Inside (or Newly Out)

Leaving—or even questioning—a high-control religion like Jehovah's Witnesses can be daunting. You may feel isolated, fearful, or unsure of where to turn. If you find yourself in this place, know there are people and communities ready to help you navigate the uncertainties and heal from the trauma of leaving. Here are a few resources to get you started:

Online Communities

Reddit: r/exjw
A large, active community of former Jehovah's Witnesses sharing stories, advice, and support. Reading others' experiences can help you feel less alone and more empowered.

JWfacts
(www.jwfacts.com)
Offers clear, documented information about Jehovah's Witness doctrine, history, and practices—helpful for those wanting factual clarity.

Counselling & Therapy
Look for mental health professionals or counsellors who specialise in religious trauma or cult recovery. The Religious Trauma Institute and directories of faith-informed therapists can connect you with someone who understands your background.

Local Support Groups & Meetups
Some cities have in-person or virtual groups for former Witnesses or ex-members of high-control

religions. A quick internet search for "ex-JW support group" plus your city or country can reveal helpful options.

Crisis Lines & Mental Health Hotlines
If you're experiencing anxiety, depression, or feel unsafe, don't hesitate to call a trusted mental health or crisis hotline in your area. There's no shame in reaching out for immediate, confidential support.

Books & Documentaries
Crisis of Conscience by Raymond Franz (former Governing Body member) can be eye-opening for those seeking an insider's perspective on the organisation.

Documentaries or interviews on YouTube, such as Ex-JW Critical Thinkers or Freed Minds, can offer encouragement and practical advice from others who've already walked this road.

Remember, questioning your beliefs or leaving the congregation does not make you weak—it means you're honouring your right to seek truth and protect your well-being. Many before you have taken these first steps, found authentic friendships on the other side, and discovered a deeper sense of self. You're not alone. Support, information, and community are out there, waiting for you.

About the Author

Being born into a working-class family in the eighties, Rebecca soon realised her aspirations lay outside of the factory floor. Like many creatives, Rebecca started dabbling with multiple art forms at a young age. Starting out as a writer, she decided to send herself off to the Academy of Journalism to study written media.

Her artistic endeavours stem from a sincere attempt to address issues close to her heart, spanning social justice, equality, and the nuanced dynamics of our world. Through her work, she aspires to initiate meaningful conversations, challenge societal norms, and cultivate connections that resonate on a profound level.

In addition to her creative pursuits, Rebecca is the founder of Sunday Mornings at the River, a small independent poetry press. Her goal is to craft thought-provoking literature that is accessible to all.

Beyond the realm of her creative endeavours, Rebecca also takes on the roles of a nursing assistant and activist. Fueled by a deep-seated desire to amplify the voices of the unheard, raise awareness about critical issues, and instigate positive change, she remains dedicated to making a meaningful impact.

About the Publisher

Sunday Mornings at the River is a poetry publisher that is dedicated to elevating and amplifying the voices of poets who are often marginalized or overlooked by the traditional publishing world.

At Sunday Mornings at the River, we are committed to creating a thriving literary community that is based on healthy and inclusive collaborations. We believe that everyone has the right to be heard, and we strive to provide a platform for poets to share their work with a wider audience.

Our focus is on publishing poetry that is thought-provoking, challenging, and that speaks to the unnameable aspects of the human experience. We believe that poets have the power to name the frauds, take sides, start arguments, and shape the world, and we are always on the lookout for new voices that are pushing the boundaries of traditional poetry.

As an independent publisher, we are dedicated to promoting equality and inclusivity in all our endeavours. Whether we are working with established authors or helping emerging poets to get their work out into the world, we are committed to creating a welcoming and supportive environment for poets of all backgrounds and experiences.

Scan me
for more books
by Sunday Mornings
at the River

w: sundaymorningsattheriver.com
e: hello@sundaymorningsattheriver.com
ig: @sundaymorningsattheriver

www.ingramcontent.com/pod-product-compliance
Lightning Source LLC
LaVergne TN
LVHW030324070526
838199LV00069B/6551